*The Full Night Still
in the Street Water*

UNIVERSITY OF NEVADA PRESS / RENO & LAS VEGAS

p o e m s

Brian Young

*The Full Night Still
in the Street Water*

❧ This project is supported
by funding from the National
Endowment for the Arts.

Western Literature Series
University of Nevada Press, Reno,
Nevada 89557 USA
Copyright © 2003 by Brian Young
All rights reserved
Manufactured in the United States
of America
Design by Carrie House
Library of Congress Cataloging-in-
Publication Data
Young, Brian, 1959–
The full night still in the street water:
poems / Brian Young.
p. cm. — (Western literature series)
ISBN 0-87417-534-8 (pbk. : alk. paper)
I. Title. II. Series.
PS3625.095 F85 2003
811'.6—dc21   2002012291
The paper used in this book meets the
requirements of American National
Standard for Information Sciences—
Permanence of Paper for Printed Library
Materials, ANSI Z39.48-1984. Binding
materials were selected for strength and
durability.

FIRST PRINTING
12 11 10 09 08 07 06 05 04 03
5 4 3 2 1

For Jenny

Contents

Acknowledgments

Some of these poems have appeared in the following magazines, to whose editors grateful acknowledgment is made: ACM (*Another Chicago Magazine*), *AGNI*, *American Letters and Commentary*, *Arshile*, *Chicago Review*, *Colorado Review*, *Denver Quarterly*, *Epoch*, *Fence*, *Grand Street*, *Gulf Coast*, *Interim*, *Iowa Review*, *N/Formation*, *Phoebe*, *Sonora Review*, *Third Coast*, and *Volt*.

One

Head

And the other thing
about this gift you've sent
It has taken the life of a customer
and drained the village of all enthusiasm
Those who had landed here
and set up their cradles
in 3-Happiness Park
with the sun chained to a tree

The air plain and pacific
now that we believed it
With an orange bird
that came on a paper plate
Other choices were:
demons all around at times,
unwound, flashy, or the monument
telling of a betrayal overheard nearby

To be memorized in several ways
while a somnambulant angel
stirs in the green palm
of your drink
It talks to itself
It tears off the tropics
The tense unremembered
Fold your flag within, it says,

And each feeling fraught with eternity
feels out another

And I'm still wearing the head
that I picked up in the last country.

3

To Accuse Someone of Something

So, that was quite an experience.
It made your eyes gleam, and the bread soft.
It made the rest of the evening's program
seem bearable. It was overpriced, of course,
but who cares now that we're in bed
with a bottle of Scotch.

Something like a new reality, it seemed,
was beginning to exist. Even if it was
only the one we'd found in being able
to refrain from admitting who we really were.
As you spend another long afternoon at the dogtrack.
And it's like poking your eyes out when you win.

The array of flashing numbers has let you relax,
and the clouds haven't moved all day.
And now it's as though I can see through
to the monstrous depths of the viral world
swirling all about, standing at the hot-dog stand
without any change, and later on again without change.

Lunar New Year

My God, what is it now? I know it can't be
all that important. You balanced the irresistible
flames in the thought of a few birds,
the makeshift eyeball, and the ceremonial screech
of a reverse sky. They are out there right now,
they are asking you to delete this, for Christ's sake.
They are made whole by the piano, played in the drugstore.
I know that nearly anything could serve as a purpose
in your life now. In the arbitrary connections
of the late afternoon, without a radiating hedge
to dream by. It is fascinating to watch
the trains arriving, unloading the pig-tarts
and the red-peppers, in a continually unbroken dawn
that has been chewed upon by a purple and pristine mirage,
the locals on fire, the shellfish sky,
and blue coffee of an intangible romance
as the planet spins its rocks and streams
in and out of view, or lately, in the nutmeg forest,
the animal without its own conception to arrange,
unremembered between martinis and the cubism
of your violently green eye.

Underground Beach

I.

If any arise, disoriented,
and the world like a working field
held out, holding baby formula, ceremoniously.
I can't believe what they're doing to each other.
What devotion toward the hard, striking branches in the rain.
"Let us worship and fall down."
Grandiloquent fever, as we stand and surrender
to the slovenly leaves, eat the rose wildly and vanish,
like crosses when he comes climbing out of God's mouth,
and came to be what they claimed at once.
But what can't be had in the moment as it opens up?
"But lay up treasure for yourselves," preserve the farm,
pass out from beyond all understanding, evermore
a ruler.

2.

I've seen the way people climb out of themselves
and onto the thorns, looking for a way of not knowing
what to expect, and to make it beautiful.
To think of themselves as buried treasure
and to say: "I treasure you."
What is it that makes the pine (the spine) fly?

Red peppers and the fisted sun.
A silver tree that came onto the morning sky.
We want to be whole.
We've gone down to the basement with our applications.

Syringes and these gentle horses bite the sweet ground.
So the miracle chain.
So it be discreet in the severity of its doing.
So it makes you feel like nothing is ever going to change.

3.
Science-fiction clouds against a throbbing, slaughtering
sky coming at you and blown up in critical attire.

It was you who conceived of the project we found ourselves in
like a box-office smash in the sunlight.

We came wearing our names backward to carry off the silver tree.
Then in the refined cell, sinking.

Disposable Chinese Camera, 24 Shots

She came back off
the broken land
wearing a Dodgers jersey
and fondling a stick,

she said that they had become
accustomed to being
attacked by stray dogs,

and that nothing was really
worth a forehead on this corner.

Each painted corner sits
on a seedy tongue
with no patience,

and the filthy river
carries a truth we could never
have dreamed when the years
had passed themselves off

like muttering alcoholics
on its radiant surface.

Maybe the trade on that river
put a meatball in our soup.

It was of no use to me
in the wild cacophonic breeze,

though you may come to be.

I'm still as smooth as new glass
in the evenings,

when the leaf falls out of your mouth.

And if I could make it clearer,
maybe I would,
or maybe you would,

but I'm afraid I left the camcorder
in my father's trunk
and the tape is covered with salt.

Half your life as it simultaneously
would be now is his,

and I've only got photos
from a disposable Chinese camera
of a petty thief that still may shimmer
or shiver in the partial dawn,

feel this golden rain in your face
like the rhyme in your reasoning,

feel it tearing down whatever it is
that thinks it is waiting for you,
as the growth on each day
demands that you feel it, or does it?

I suppose it's different, at any rate,
than wanting to live it and make of it
what it would've been anyway
but for the steel towers,

the cool hammers lighting up the bars,
and a cock that leaves off
in a loner's sleeping mouth
with beta-leaves.

I couldn't stop.
I didn't know what to do.
I played an old house tape.
Then I played the "This Old House" tape.

9

Its succulent burden
hunkers down
as the mask of memory
in one reactionary pose,

it's the user's manual
flipping open in a bay window
at 4th and California
above the Chiyo Beauty Salon

torn from a page of purple sky
beneath the full moonie trees in deep summer,

and all the other tenants,
though naturally abject
from licking up the lack as tenderness,
soundly doped to sleep now,

uncoiling their spirits from the T
of a dumb and darkening history.

(This landscape has been with me for days now,
an inarticulate beast spewing forth bad sculpture.

I spent most of the morning
"looking at the receipts."

All of these insects have blown into the room,
knowing that "someday never comes."

And when I turn on this "notebook,"
it sounds like a radiation detector,

and a folded part
of the world disappears

just as we're saying "God"
or "the hard nipples in the machine.")

So we went into the city and spun
with the spinning circles of reference.

In fact, it seemed like it was overloaded
with referentiality,
and this made us wonder if we should have
viewed ourselves

as having been there at all,
or just the ad sheet
blowing down the street
with recreant abandon,

or Janet speaking into the tape recorder
with the winter colors on her back:

It was only the way we'd hoped to see one another,
without all this freakishness doctoring the moment.

And I laugh
and I get skewed.

I close my eyes for a second
and a neon pagoda appears.

A sunbather is steadily approaching us
with a syringe in her ankle.

One throaty horse over on
the lawny prospect.

Evening will come and mutter:
It's a grave with a glass eyeball in it.

Belief wander conjure.

"Just give me the originals and stop worrying."

Extraordinary little girl
in a hand so extraordinarily evil.

Placed beneath the cherry blossoms
in a plaid dress to listen.

To our supercilious songs:
Spring raving wildly about.

"Everyone wants to process
these Chinese chemicals but no one can."

Janet with her tape recorder,
"Who's getting fucked beneath the blue stars?"

"Memory hardens each
upon a considerably cheaper impulse?"

He'll heel heal.

Low abandoned hills in the glass hours.

These are just two tickets
to a movie about a sunburn.

Beijing Beer

1.
A drunk wants the spicy fish soup
and to insist that there is only one God,

not to become dispersed, O Lord,
into chronological conditions of strain and distress.

A lifetime largely reconstituted, the recorded seashore,
the burning stables, the absolute brink of excess,

large government grants, a clown's cerebellum soaked
upon the celebrated tower, and stuffed full of salami.

The elimination of compelling narratives,
and a self-tanning mentality to disfigure the moon with,

to take a jackhammer to the vegetable garden
without any pressure to get the job done before dawn.

Only to recall what once was or may have been,
to project it in the tones that were given, and given over

as Miriam grabs the tambourine and the sweet potatoes,
her head looking new against the buttered gate.

Will the cause of monotheism be advanced?
The subcontractors all feel a little threatened?

To be lewd, to be habitual.
Retranslated, what a deranged smirk it has.

2.
Then you realized that it was you that this was
happening to, and not always as someone else.

All your life then, tapped on the shoulder by a grass hand,
or someone with fake binoculars staring out the window.

Then it may be an ornithologist's "then."
The whole alignment so totally fucked-up,
and the cedar waxwing veering off to the right.

Just the exultation of it.
Out of the cane reliquary, it will return the wall
upon us, and the bushes will spin again with Chevrolets.

3.
And this, it is hoped, will sustain us,
if it can deliver them wholly and with a fine touch

of sanctimony into the enameling realm of the extraordinary,
and divide us up, and it doesn't matter

what it leads you to think
or talk about, as you already know,

as though you were capable of making some effort
to be serious, even if you may in fact
have some kind of a life in place somewhere,

and if not really "in place," then in Arizona,
where you've been lounging around with a wet fist
since the fall of Saigon, rolling some

tobacco and using the cherry-scented porta-johns
lined up on the sidewalk on festival days,

which can be numerous if you think repeatedly
about them, though it's true that many people fail to,

but still, it is hoped that a few
harmless delusions will fall to you each day,

like wine through your corn flakes
and into the sleeves of the mindless sun.

Exactly Twelve Hours of Light or So

All day long, ordering refills of Lorazepam.
Dr. Vowel Erasure Hole
in the American cereal.

That's where we are again today,
beneath a grainy old photograph of Lake Superior.

Boiling some hot dogs in the tapwater for lunch,
a headless chicken's breast for dinner, some dolmades,
all in the unceasing jar of behaviorisms.

Who's to say you've been left without your lucky Christ?
Or Gen'l Hirohito, the wiener dog, yelping in your lap?

All day long, ordering refills of Clonazepam.
The goat swallows the grass and vertigo.

All day long, ordering refills of Diazepam.
Sunset and privilege so ambient.

A small head with a sticker that reads "Ambien"
pressed against it.

Enunciated with elasticity.
The rain on the leaves lustrous and parenthetical.

Just to be near the window in autumn, the muddy day
slowing down, without one clear idea
to come down: quaking aspen, census, heart of palm.

Creation Theory in the Schools

When your face fills a shade in the rippling water
and the wind unbuckles belief in the doctor
the branches sheathed in ice remind you
how much surface area there is in the world

and the wind unbuckles belief in the doctor
at the rickety tavern on the corner
how much surface area there is in the world
near the factory smoke, red-tinged at sunset

at the rickety tavern on the corner
everyone taking antidepressants and getting together
near the factory smoke, red-tinged at sunset
until the cash register beheads one lover, and then another

everyone taking antidepressants and getting together
in gale-force winds, whole trees will start to move
until the cash register beheads one lover, and then another
getting angry over nothing, old bricks, perfect moon

in gale-force winds, whole trees will start to move
the wellness center sitting atop the bent flowers
getting angry over nothing, old bricks, perfect moon
which is so much of what it wants to be
              beyond what you meant it to be

the wellness center sitting atop the bent flowers
when your face fills a shade in the rippling water
which is so much of what it wants to be
              beyond what you meant it to be
the branches sheathed in ice remind you.

Beautification

I know what you're thinking
It isn't pretty
There are mass-murderers in the margins

I've put the glossies on the ground
Down there with your complaints swirling in the dust

Still something had to be done
After all this is Pioneer Park

But really it's okay to welcome the moon
The way you do
So abstractly as though originally

Argument with Sugar

I kept repeating it to myself
in order to give it meaning,
and though you know that
it's a waste of time,

You want to eat more of it
and what it might have to say,
as the dripping evening wears away
in its torn butcher's smock

As we come to realize
that we are nothing but
a collection of images
in reverse, and they eat us,

And all that we thought
we knew was that it was
better, surely, not to
question yourself too much,

And that if you don't
maybe no one else will either,
here in the beckoning paradise
of shiny fruit, in this sky

That's about to spin
its tape, so that
the gently rolling hills
can luxuriate in the rain,

and you will be frying
dreamily in space.

Morning in Iowa

Taking in the flickering sun
and sucking each other off,
toward the spinning new day
as it comes to fill up
the nervous trees,

for one thought that may
leave you with a different name
come autumn, when the headsets
fill with astonishing leaves,
and the river

is bright with glistening birds
and poppers, just as we are
throwing the windows here open
on a windy pricey day,

knowing that nothing was ever
what we meant it to be
when we saw it,

but it is, nevertheless, there,
and it does stop to wait for you,
one place or another.

Summer Tanager

1.
It is very green now, that is agreed,
now that it is June. But I also have green
sunglasses on. There is a new bird
glittering in the tree and I think it

is a summer tanager. It is summer after all,
on nothing but the day going by,
civility and its serious lantern,
the whole concept corrupted in the freaky tulips,

in the postcard of the wax president
that cleaves to the innocuous watercolors
while reading the *Weekly World News*
and ordering the rigatoni in the shopping mall,

the posters of cantaloupe in plain view,
having come to be the reason
we thought of the limitless breakage,
the deft adjustment, and the luck of it.

2.
Before the moon can bite the railway ties,
the sky a deep-blue contracting ring,
the cardinal crests municipally
on the white oak branch, and comes singing

without the complexity of a stolen experience,
sundown converting the breast feathers
of a cliff swallow, or your victim of it,
not enough love to keep the hideous screen off you,

the contact in you, the self-esteem over there
with desire for the planet, for a vine
like Pericles and his nipple ring, the nation
backed into a skylight marvels at the howling day,

weeping for the maple in an ideological hour,
then asleep in our awful and sound achievements,
rising without any sense or doubt, doctored
to delight in worthless modifications,

finding the right place to register and feeling
preposterous but clean to the sound of the organ
which laments in lovely reddish tones
that clear out the captioning upon us

for the vendors, the sound crew, and the caretakers
at the wellness center, spending the discount day
planting corn at the gas station with a hill
behind us, the maples torn by the cruel winds

and mannerisms, the disintegrating work truck
in the sad Memphis of your heart, to be wasted
all over again in the contours of the great station
and know you're going somewhere, to be generous

with our opinions, but stingy with our liquor,
a clean sweep for the lavender sky that wasted us
on the way home with just some broccoli
and red potatoes, a sort of fallout lavender

at sundown with blue and gray breast feathers
and municipal sex on the street, near the sign,
on the radio, the bent stars and a bag full
of bright oranges, the feeble pandemonium

of goatsuckers in the acid rain, the kids selling
peanut brittle, and the clumps of grass falling
through our fingers, so what if it rains in the park
and the savagery of the moment is just opening up?

Mix a strange drink, and notice the asters and druggists
near the police van as it participates with the killer
before the full complexity of the company is uncovered,
the killer that slept by the river,

known by empty, empty paintings
of payday, payday, payday,
a room broken down into the light on polished apples,
it flashes like a momentary nation in a searchlight.

Into the Previously Dying Wind

1.
We went back into the segment on the river-lights,
near the highway construction, these lights layering
each other and causing the muscles in our eyes to conflict
and adulate, near the last few minutes of the sun

smashing the windows;
this is the place you dreamed of,
burned down on the spur of the moment.

Water the cornfield.
800 million strangers.

A patrolman breaking a face
like a metal cloud.
36 floors of campsites.
Look for a barn with an X on it.

2.
It would have seemed too magical
to leave the car in the pond.
After getting directions
and having breakfast in the pear trees.
Watching you walk across the footbridge
without your medication.
Taking pictures like a cereal box
of the heartland.

Scrawny dogwood by the road.
Punished in its lavender and ambivalence.
Wearing the blackbirds of our suicidal God.
As though everything was very uncommercial-like.

3.
You will know us by our having known what to say
to the doctor in order to get the medication

we wanted, to make the towering gift of the maple shine,
the way it will twist a Pizza Hut into place

beneath the huge ideological nude of the October sky,
and as it moves itself up against you, making you feel
holy and fucked brainless in the discount pond, quivering
as though you were actually in the moment, left behind

like the bound swan of the service, in the restless
critique of the sun, the burning trees, the hawk floating
through the bright container on the grassy side of memory
which we lost relaying the right symptoms to the doctor,

going out of the door and into the ashes, out of the bank
that belched out the tractors and pigs that dreamt
of snowy pens, and kept the duck the doctor bent
from demonstrating the exterior light, like a footnote

that has been xeroxed into a smear and can't be read,
when all you really did was ring the wrong doorbell
and we've been listening to the same tape since we left
Muscatine, Iowa; where we searched around for food

but couldn't find any in the colossal shadows
of the refineries by the river as the snow began to stick,
and being unable to sell ourselves for a simulator, we were
appropriated on a whim, into the previously dying wind.

4.
After the lavender tree was beaten,
we flew to ourselves,
to be read to like a cave with its fire on,
to be sent by the ambiguity,

or sent by the boss,
even after she's dead, to be sent
to recover her pattern of receipts,
and the fields already under water.

5.
Let's go back and disappoint the experience that claimed
to be ours. It itself strains to be released from you
and your idea of it. The accumulation of events, and the colors
that qualify them. The pain coming as that part of perception

which is forced upon your perspective by distance.
We are its halting objects, and you may want to feel
yourself up against it, dreamless in the municipally brainless
and discount shade. The swallows spread the morning out

in a fast blue while you're defrosting the refrigerator,
finding chickpeas and spinach. We were asked to get imaginary
with these tractors, shining variously, like investment
portfolios. That is why the sun rolls down the trees

toward the vague notion of a convertible being ticketed
by the Temple of Mere Fragments. Awake now with the new
carrots and dismantling the smoke detector. Saving enough
time to think about being somewhere else, out there

on the land that spins its strange brain
before going out, beneath another part of the sky
that rises knowingly on your makeup and easel,
shaped with reference to this and then that,

that sky is electrical and complete,
it rains so that no one has to starve,

we were disoriented, so we beat the tree,
and it felt like we flew to ourselves.

Two

Cars

1.
Cruising into the full-blown
radiating breast feathers
of dawn's willing victim,

you're a doll
and you'll be free now,

with a grassy knoll,
ready to share
your brain with everyone.

2.
Without a head to sleep in,
night swings her airplane.
You won't play God,
and you're not free now.

3.
We like to get smashed
in the mountains.

Clouds Like Flying Saucers

It's hilarious how I just drive down
this same road every day after work.
Because it's perfectly straight and takes me
right home past the ideal trees in the new park.

This backyard barbecue has such balance.
I feel peculiar, but not really theatrical
toward the repetition of the flagrant, fragrant hours
spent returning phone calls, unable to remember

the names of birds, or those colors coming undone
for flight, or the direction of the sweet river
in the lives of outsiders. Whatever happens to us,
we believe, and breathe into ourselves as belief,

like that bird soaring in the iced-out sky, or eye,
or "fist-fucking." What do I mean? I can't seem to remember
what anyone wanted, or why? I know that the mail came,
and I forgot. I anticipate that. Someone got fired

and she was crying. I thought about all
the singular moments that must go into one starvation.
Then I had to be at the meeting. The wind was insane,
clouds like flying saucers.

A Letter to "Someone with Railroad Tracks"

Though we love you dearly, and call you,
through our glaciated teeth, "the west,"
the rippling eye that shifts in the wind,
then in succession, no one seems to have noticed
a young girl being sharpened on the sidewalk,
then in succession. This was just
the way we stood around humming a tune
beneath the iron sky, and could it always be just
as simple as changing heads, just as we
had always been told, and could we be just
as sweet and phony beneath a different sun?

Would the meaningless then interrupt at the same intervals,
and come from the same sort of idiotically radiating faces?
Does it come with what you have thought, and what that has
thought of you? Does it open up like a blue eye in the 19th
century, saying: Just what the hell do you mean, anyway?

Just like that moron who is shouting from beneath a tree,
and as he continues to construct something, a future
or an alibi, a tape is inserted into the player, and it
further enlivens him, and he berates himself for the words
"naughty little girl" that rise each night from his sleep,

and which bring him here each day to destroy these gentle
red saplings, the fisted dream that has given them a name,
and the sky is but a handful of shellfish: Though it will
make nothing happen, it will leave nothing unsaid either.

But this was going to be a letter.
The germs here are strong and I'm drinking
a little bourbon as a challenge to them.
I'm holding onto the bottle, the cheap label,
and I can feel the tender and tormenting glow

begin to shine from the contents inside, and know
that it always has, and that as it magnifies,
it couldn't possibly have promised more,
just before the strange light will begin to turn
itself around, just as you begin to think:
I won't say anything more.
Except that I thought I already had.

Plagiarism at Dawn

There's an acrylic chair wavering
in the foreground like an extra cup of coffee,

the added sponsor picked up
after the last few leaves of the year

have filled the bowl
you lick without much provocation,

knot what's there,
knot the mirage we stumbled upon,

renting first for an hour
on the unformulated beach,

then succumbing to and drifting off
into its essentiality as it heaped
exaggeration upon exaggeration within us,

even if it was only the elaborate sex—
suspended by the ankles from the antique rafters—
we thought we might be imagining later in the day,

after some arrangements had been made,
and you could feel at ease inside the blue peppers,
and I am less human than you, and our desires, it seems

must become more and more complicated in order to have the
potential for finding us interested, yet this complexity,
the angels of Chrysler treading above the blue summer pond,
at the same time seems to trivialize us, in that it often
seems to be no more than our conformity to ourselves, or
just the need to get to Raven and 3rd from here, which is
always somewhat tricky because of the one-way streets, as

though you had begun again to feel this way toward yourself
simply because of the paint on the walls of this place, a
garish replica of the sky at dusk in the Midwest, October,

or as though you were really about to begin again
to have trouble deciding if that box of bricks over there
was your elementary school or your detox clinic,

as though you could stop mispronouncing your minute
of winter light as easily as you can erase your name,
and fix forever in the shade, on the hour,

but look, I know that it had originally been me
who had approached you on the bus about all of this,
it was a sort of totalitarian thing for me to do, I know,

it was a manipulation of many things,
not the imagination least of all,
at least not in retrospect,

but if it takes all day just to wake up,
and most of that is spent in your need to worry about it,
then it's just someone else's life in your observatory,

which is all I've ever really had to say, maybe I meant it,
maybe the light as it fell on the sad customers with their
credit histories was just the way you described it, maybe
there was a way to fix on some pure sound, or at least
the idea of it, and that it may have let us go off and go
bright green in as many different directions as we could
have pleased, but maybe there is no conceivable way for me
to get to the Travel Bar tonight, that as I'm writing this
the sky buries its wet moon in clouds, and it sounds like
someone is coughing to death down there on Division:

Plymouth

These trees are the wild and twisted red shades
of our lost daughters, limitless is the motion
above the graves, as the sky recoils for winter,
and the fluctuating afternoons beyond the unceasing
and perfect water, the remnant of sky where the crow chokes,
the fingering blackout that waits in the east,
and we aren't really here in these names
we've broken open, as the sky chews on your shining cherry,
and the god which is said to inhabit the hideous dream
of architecture, and the control box which is killing me,
it kills me when you breathe with me.

Recollection

I was walking out of the bookstore
and tying you to another tree,

and how do you look?

I'm biting you on the neck
and now on each nipple,
and I think you might like it,

you seem to be glowing,
to be getting more and more marginal.

Ever wait around
for something significant to happen?

Better yet, pure insignificance.
Pearlescent trees all turning in your head
as they were said to be,

voice out of nowhere
repeats a room full of wet stars,
rose petals radiating idiosyncratically,

they are the same, we are,
I kiss you, it seems all right.

You're naked and tied to a tree,
like a shallow half-moon in cherry dynamite,

and the light falls out of place,
changes its dress,
it has texture and it holds us in place,

I bite your neck,
I like sucking your cunt,
falling off the wagon, that's as if

the other name were to leave,
and it's no accident,
or if it is, who cares?

You're sweet and drugged up,
"you are lost and gone forever,"

everything is shining,
though it doesn't seem to be
anything like real description
here on this weird planet,

"if the names of wild birds
in your mouth mean wet birds,"
then it's good to drink them.

I like sucking your astrological cunt,
and the light you are,
it rises over us, it holds us
in one wavering place,

and you bite me on the shoulder,
eyes like hard blue nipples,
your hair falls over my face,
your fingers are warm,

you look at me, kiss me again,
and bite one of my nipples,

lip to lip the sky turns
us over in different colors,

the west is dripping wildly
with the blood of Jesus,
you're wet and breathing,
and you're doing it now.

I like talking to you.
I'm biting on this piece of rubber.
But I wish I could see you now,
and be here.

Will you suck my cock?
Your eyes are clear, will you fuck me
with the moonlight on your back?

Do you think there is a strange
and benevolent god of discipline
that feeds the supernatural
into our discovery?

Just as we can taste the new leaves
on the tree being lashed with a whip?

Whose slave was here and were we
when we weren't listening?

And is this the way that we are kept
imagining it before the return
to our names leaves us
unable to feel it again?

As we were about to say
that it would go on unnoticed,
scraping our knees on the wild grass,
knowing that it's real,

there's a trance in it,
and it's growing between your legs,

it's the rain feeling us up,
and it's dripping
from your hands, nipples, and needles,
it leaves that red sky rolling in my mouth,

I bite you on the ass, it's good to be
whipped like this, you want to fuck me
with a burning candle, my back is burning
and I can't see well, my shoulder feels sore,

you're holding my head in your hands,
turning it around to face you,
and it is explicit wire, it's all
one tower and it's looking at me, so?

So, you're chewing on the soft moon,
and the branches are still wet,
you whip them again and bite me

on the neck; hey, it's only gender,
will you go for a ride with me?
Up to the Painted Rocks?

Bite your clit, kiss, feet on the wet earth
and moving again, the bushes seeming greener
than ever; it's great, we're feeling lazy and safe,

no one is around trying desperately to be heard,
we're just stopping here and lying out
in the warm sun, it's going to sink.

69 No Reflection Avenue

I.

The morning is being eaten by the rain
and rubs its ghost against a falling eye.

It hangs a nail upon the radiating tower
and slows the park to a tranquil heartbeat.

It releases the roots from thirsting
in the rising, carnal light that comes
with red-throated birds that hinge upon
the verge of remembrance, as the sun
carries off the bed before the sky
can call itself back into a September
of blazing sumac. So dear was the land
how we dreamt it, so gently without a brain
the fruit falls open, and the language
shimmers in the yellow leaves. The wired
leaves that spill off the hours on a day
that is a tender tongue spreading azaleas
over the airwaves, that marks each
nipple for terror, for the tremor in each
abused eye, to simply pull a tangerine
out of the sweet atmosphere, and vanish.

2.

Radiating in the fictional tower,
with love from time to time, I'd see you
opening up in the mirroring field,
bearing the blue satellites and the cash
we squandered in the singing room, or
leaving the idiotic woods to sing
without us, you'd keep to the delight,
however artificially, and the planets
would come, to be near you, and fixed.

And a star collapsed in the cocktail lounge.

Without waiting for us to fade into that
loving aimless mind so treasured for the way
it never was, but is worn and savagely bound
to the Christmas speakers that blare and leave
a globe burning in your mouth. Or the promise
of one that had merely been a conjecture
of the glass sun, a glinting, ghastly stem
lowered into the distress of 12 billion strangers.

3.
I have eaten so many unbelievably strange things now,
"without hearing the voice that beautifies the land,"
but no doubt it has tangled itself within you,
and left you with only your national cord for hope.

And is that what is breaking out of the mire
of your malleability? Out of the corner of your eye?
Is that which has claimed us anything like us at all?
Was it there in the water that we prayed for,
and could you say that it had any feeling for us?

In the "giving in"? In the blankness that accompanies
submission, in anything we desire and nothing ever
willing to be the same? These musical spirits that can
lift the hours off a merely categorical memory of a glen
that was moderately beautiful despite the empty 12-packs.   **41**

We sought this motion yearly
and dazzling birds on the shoreline.

—A man walked out of the drugstore
    and asked me to take a picture of him
    walking out the drugstore—I thought it was

sort of disgraceful but not really
so important—
I shot him, quickly—

Or, when the motorcade was carrying the Pope to the stadium,
and the blue jays were landing on the romantic billboard,
graceful and freshly painted, was it all simply the fact
that the chances were slim that anyone would be unwilling
to go unnoticed? Or was the setup much more sinister?

In any case, we sought to polish off the remaining moments
by going overboard with the inward, toward recognizing
that nature has a way of forgetting itself when it comes
near you, and that as the light was pulled down each day,
I meant to memorize the 12-pack glen as a response,

but it was useless
and didn't seem to exist at all,

the hotels came on momentarily
and the dogs became strange.

4.
We left ourselves in the scarlet copies
of the soft, nude evening, in the sky

that wished to have you this way,
and was waiting for you to notice,

in the simulation of boats
changing in a fog,

you drank the gin
that decorated the swans

which were amazed and floated
over to be near you.

A Chatterbox in the Aspirin Trees

1.

It is not, of course, so strange to see someone asleep
as it is to see them awake, and looking for an empty seat
on this train, with bread, plums, and the shadow
off the Basilica, the ripe tomato on your white belly,
the full moon in your pussy, which shines on the lives
we led, and it keeps flipping back to an edited entry
on day-breaking paper, something we may still believe
though it's eaten into shade a little more each day,
and evening is altogether blank, though splendid as rain
on spring leaves, or the ambulance that is racing away,
and there is a feeling that is so sinister and contrived
attached to this idea of heaven, and it is too easy for me
to feel my identity giving way, just as the soft cement
rolls off the conveyor belt and into the river, where
the ducks have done their breeding, and the whole family
has gathered to gaze, though it seems that the water
may have lost most of its meaning in direct proportion
to our loss of memory, and I don't think I've ever seen
a sky that looked so much like a painting, the cathedral
has rinsed itself in dark clouds and ancient domination
to meet it, and to make you want it, and what it meant
when that sky was inexhaustible, and done in oils.

2.

Tearing a hard nipple on the bark of a bonsai tree: 43
"It's much brighter than this," or that is, or
whatever gets done in our having you to do it,
in the enchanting posters of the serial trees
that gave a kind of meaning to life on this corner,
the full television blaring in your dry mouth,
and the kids glowing with "the day" that pours
from its monthly payment eye, the body that wants
to be borrowed by the mirror, and believe in the land
surely enough to sleep tonight, and let the passion

of the earth subside with a bowl of cold cabbage soup,
which lowers us into the strange quality of the night
as it is reflected in the faces of those who have lost
track of what it was they once meant, how their days
at the beach had been full of the most unlikely
and beautiful behaviorisms, and I, too, had once been
very busy, and the helicopters had kept me ambitious,
but then, it seemed, the rules hadn't changed so much
as become clear, and my ambitions only served to lift
the machines, the branches flew away as the days mangled
themselves upon returning, and the local administrators
put up a sign saying: "This way to an even nicer park,
to you alter-Oisin, and the tangerine tea."

3.
Then we began to realize that we had been raising children
who were even more stupid than the television shows
they liked to watch, and we all lay back in our separate
daybooks, and tuned to the sycamores we'd sold for a song
about heaven, and this tape continues to play on
in the wide-open spaces, as each day comes fully apart
to wear its roses, feed the dogs, and burn from that TV
which is full of flags and freeways all transhormonally bright.

We took the remaining land
out of the safe
and burned it,
then, accidentally, we looked
out the window and nothing came back.

So, I went back to make sense of it, and that was a mistake,
this desire to have it make sense for you instead of for me,
that and allowing everything to merge into functionality,
and when our ashes were laid beside us in the cauldron,
this meal we were seemed like it had already been going on
forever, and was it meant to imply that it was not so
strange that this should have happened? As the mere thought
of the supercilious doctor had suggested that it might?

The guide we were
told to study
claimed that some exotic birds
had never really even existed.

4.
Registering for something once, we watched a woman
pound a staple into her index finger, and we knew then
that another's pain was unknowable, and appearances
became more irritating than ever, and we wanted her

to hurry with our paperwork, and the man beside her
winced with a face full of rubies, as though the moths
had completely exhausted themselves inside him, so we went
back to the meditation dome to be bolstered by the stiff

bravery of each new hymn, and the believable products there
in plain view would suck the land off its nerve-wracking
reverberations, and hold us over through the company songs,
which would calm us, those lovely tunes and the river

that made the wind leap over this quiet town, though it seemed
that each betrayal came off more casually than the last,
though they were all conceived of in an identical
parking structure, near the waiter who continually droned,

"You bring the beer this time . . . Forever . . ."

5.
. . . in the aspirin trees, with a vein to share.

For a thought coming back to be its shell only,
the ridiculous questions that caused us
to call out for the well-being of the company,
and to collapse at a bar in space.

6.
In the shadow of The One-Star Hotel,
I splashed my face against the fifth wall.

7.
We came out of the surf,
and everything seemed to have changed,
though the distortion is all the same
to the listeners calling in,

calling for the destruction
of yet another bewildered nation,
to the distress of 12 billion cypress trees,
"and thrush through the echoing timber,"

so I'll leave a glass brain
to turn in the medieval shade,
and turn toward the vegetable stand
in the triangular shadows that hang heavily,

and stick to the terrific argument
called "human nature," though it's not one
I'm really trying to win here,
or even make as much sense with

as I think you might want, but no one is
made utterly voluntary by this fountain
with the yearning nude statues,
and only an idiot can laugh

without turning back the sky,
without ever having had to
fall asleep in the park,
out beneath the leather arch.

8.
So you're found in a different sequence
in a separate, though similar park,

having been rewound without the slightest concern
for your feelings, and being forced
to listen to the bastard idiot
in the presidential cap, and the passion
with which he bites off his sister's clitoris
before attending the convention
wearing his speech like a costume.
He claims to have been confused,
or deceived by the bankers near the lake,
or that not enough stars fell to him
as he stood out in the cornfield
with the children that were praying.

And I think I must have been dead after all,
I can't remember anything coming next.

I'm just standing out here,
surrounded by fireflies.

9.
I like my apartment to look a little bit like a campsite,
I thought I heard myself saying,
and I would like this interview so much more
if this interviewer wasn't really here,
or anywhere, or maybe just the wrong line
in the long, dark book,
wherein the earth is continually
likened to a machine,
the way it will roll a field with wildflowers
off of its smooth conveyor belt,
and set them beneath
your broken, tired feet.

10.
We came out of the surf,
and everything seemed to have changed,
yet when morning comes again
and shines upon the metal leaves,

the distortion will be all the same
to the listeners calling in,
calling for an end to "sublunary vice,"
though the menu can offer nothing else,
to recreate you, "and thrush
through the echoing timber,"
and this can still make the hills waver
when you name them, though it is hard
to recall what it was, exactly,   ·
that we expected one another to mean, or be,
as the song seemed to have tangled
several birds in the air, and let you be
lost for a few moments in a fading detail,
worn into the hillside with a bottle of wine,
while the sky fell upon its bloody knees,
and made you smile, the pharmacy that opened
from within its wide gash, and the power lines
that always got lost there when you looked for them,
in that very same crushed and lazy sky,
wandering into the Museum of the Categorical Heart,
bemused and drunk, and though you'd known
that the power lines were important,
you were still unprepared for the snobbery
that was apparent at The Festival Held
to Adore Them and to Adorn Them.

Carbon County

Sets out, on the plains of vagary
and calling down a remote shell for velocity,
how resolute the abandoned self,
and the jinx of it all, the whimsical cranes
raise the bells on my sleeve, and the short
duration of my accomplice's futurity

The night split, spilt and spelt down
      the postures of futurity, its feudal posters
The futility it awoke to recede
      into mass vagary, the virgins in the lemon verbena
      unbinding
The moment it took to blaze into
      risk was not the significant moment, too unearthly,
      too short and scrumptious
I didn't have a chance, a pick, to hack up
      the question of its velocity, not that it mattered,
      the entire community being so vile, so ready to
      cooperate, so disgusting, so sickening, so what
So much construction in sight, and so
      on the lyric horizon, so many strange dogs
      sniffing around the cranes, the young Cardinal
      Liberace's mini-focaccia, tender fiend your tendrils
      tendrils
Are no real source of pleasure for anyone, least of all
      yourself, draped over the Bank of the Madonna Lily
      at dawn, reflecting upon a necro-stammering
      glittering shower of glass bugs one sultry
      and preposterous island in June and July

In our stammering we knew it meant July,
      with books about gift triangles and large quantities
      of the Brain Protector nearby, ours on display, we knew
      it meant something or nothing to the soft

boiling sunfish in the pot, and their good pink livers,
all for the beautiful sound of my pill bottles jangling
in my pocket
As we climbed into Faultline Park to get
a better view of the mammoth posters of the dewy
green meadows, and the honeybees ablaze, the only
recklessness in those imitations of others we had
inadvertently become, plowed down like sentences
beneath the hedges, the tipsiness, I said, those were
pill bottles that were his eyes, those are yours,
pill bottles multiplying so rapidly, not you
The unbinding of the batteries from their monochromatic
boxes, the scrumptious tendrils of the tornado we thought
to win to our side, each Sunday checked off
from the calendar, if it all could only mean as much
as it does, or will, the disposable lighter now low
on fuel, do I still mean to mean something to
someone when they're sleeping
The unbinding of the egrets
from the chemical spillage, they love it there so,
as though it were a pond composed of lustrous
egret-wine, and the blue finches beside the transport
glow, to all who have the time to forget the moments
as they are unmade in them, here, take this lovely
pill, my lonely chanteuse, what is

There beyond the predictable wafer?

What is it that you've spent
the last five minutes debriefing? A crane?
I've only heard it called "the originary" between hamburgers
but in that the trees were changed into chains decibels
rotator-cuff surgery I don't doubt it

Scrumptious as the same twenty-year-old lines Mr. X laid
down on the page like cocaine, for lunch, de la Con,
de la Boogie, de la instant-replay karma, its willingness

alone, its break from break to time so dear so perverse,
its weeds, it's this problem you have, it needs
a stupid surly alcoholic to survive it, to retrieve it
and install it, it's that grotesque furniture again, etc.

Country Clouds Like Flying Saucers

It's hilarious how I just drive down
to the smoky old church
of sundown since you've gone.

To spill gin for the broken-hearted.
Grainy inventions of the cottonwood trees.

Always Sunday and tilted off the unsteady shore,
the host within a banker's mind
fills these grain-breakers with teeth,

and then shakes loose the seeds of belief.

Three

Speculation Upon Happiness

Something like, or somewhere near, that
"I'm with Stupid" T-shirt.
The title of this poem is "Kicking Horse Reservoir."

Walking out of the farewell episode,
not an idea of anyone to call your own,
yet vaguely contained by them.

And the character you were on cable
could neither speak nor drink,
could only stalk to this virtual stopping point.

The title of this poem is "Meadowlark Lemon."

The name of the essay was "Irretrievable Interior."

Test Section

It was on the chair lift at The Snow Bowl
that the melting frost on the bare aspens
looked like dripping antlers
against the rocky and skewered mountainside.
We rode into the skull of that sky,
slicing up the sharp air above the notion
of the rain-soaked real, above the blank stare
of screech owls churning chain, dirt, and haze,
in the animal of traffic and the froth of war,
in the schemes beyond years of rusted wire,
and this god gone down in the grass,
this gin and the moment falling on your skin,
this green carnival I take down.
How did that pizza get there?
Out of water, inaccuracy, and a loss of context
to this method-worn mud when the width of sleep
is widening, I walk into park, self-conscious,
where the cardinal caught in the sudden
violence of the maple is released into its full
red wingspan, and stares through me,
which leaves me substituting for myself,
slicing garlic, answering to the listening machine,
or coming through the imitation door
to find you rubbing yourself all over
and chanting something incomprehensible
in order to get a job as an assistant
in the arbitrary wind that blows the yellow jackets
from tree to tree and the processed, tender numbers
that fall from a salad of diverted sky
and I suck on that part
of being the park.

Deadline

I.

Nice planet. The geese are following the river north
against the corrugated wind and rearranging digitally,
a green pressure has been applied to everything we think
we move, a fresh grave in the shade of an evergreen,
and I've walked over here, Rodina, to undo an orange and
a turkey sandwich in your stone shadow, you may know how
I feel about you and wonder, lazy there in the soundtrack
where the trees have fresh triggers budding in the warm
fist, no longer jammed-up nerve-wise, not like

the workers on the verge of existence wages sent into
the Holiday Inn lobby armed with shears and spray bottles
full of Malathion for the mealy bugs on the aspidistras,
waiting for a day when waking up means Mars matters somehow,
the pleasant low light on the water table with orange peels
and Mars candy bars, and unable to get any pleasure out
of a newspaper but where the beaver chewed and bargained
its tail against the March current, yanking itself into
the recollection of being, and you willing

to smile and wait for someone to smile back, spending hours
out in the sorghum field where the content couldn't be any
better, or sweeter, or when things get too murky, how would
you like to be a duck with a little white collar? What can
we argue with here? Here in these woods where the wiring
is new, sundown-cornered and parallel-red? It's as though
we desecrated the meaning of winter by going to hear
the strange doctor, shivering like radio static, unable
to find the numbers we need to get through, to do

the job "sorta-right," and graft, going down by the capsule
that smiles back, and unconcerned about the caption upon us,
the exact circumstance of the surrogate sky that softens
up the minute we go back to Burger King to wait out our

57

fear, for the love of any occurrence in the courtyard with
the bougainvillea licking at the corners of the tapestry
while the air-raid siren is being tested and seems like too
many pear trees at once, and between the layers of the metal
world, we ended up blaming the river for the view that was
to be found there.

2.
How unlike one another we return the calls from the compound,
eating breakfast from memory in the fire, so holy and
misunderstood was the monotony, and the children so obedient
like fliers over the hard green hills, and the magic show
went on unnoticed, so we collapsed with our headsets tuned
to the perfect sunrise, pulling on our predictability
with the gas mask of collectivity, praying for the peace
that waits in a gentle position like a businessman on an
airliner, thinking about his colorful charts, and I wonder

if he calls himself "the sturdy tree" when he showers, or
"the operation on the meadow"? I guess the tanning club
will have forgotten about me by now. I knew what I meant
when I said that the light was alive. Makes me feel sort
of sad though, and unable to call myself "the sky for now."
Now that the flames have become so outlandish with their
desires, making new walls where the old ones were, and
illuminating the perversity of the frail, is that your hand,
Lord? What were your motives? Can you show me

what matters in your open hand? Do you have a problem
with my nudity? It's time for me to get on the paper boat
and let all of your creation feel me out. Take me down
like a wet painting off your severe wall. You need me
to take your orders, don't you?

The Dead Love the Uniform

And so we left you there in the autumn leaves
letting go. Everything crossing itself out in that
far angle of fat indecision. The thrilling waterfall
in the hardening shaft of the television pours
over the newly-roped couple fucking near the red,
serialized rocks, with him using her to fuck himself
into a sort of sympathy for the amateur police-show,
but which keeps her from measuring the central static
and channeling it into the hereaftering O, into the
inevitable neologism of "return," as the headstone
is sinking with the moment of the dangling landscape,
the canyons are blown out of context, and the ruined
bride paces among the dragonflies, the rusted Corvairs,
and the fallout trees in Three-Hearted Grove.

Isn't it simply gorgeous? Wind off the wound-up moon
racing down the superannuated sky that suffers silently
for the moment you missed its flaring, two-faced smile
failing in the west. "Eat me," snarls the two-faced
apple in an unedited section of the sudden headwind,
burning for the hybrid sun, as the sky shines furiously
toward a revision in which all the oaks are overworked
in the hard, concentrated light that slams down
and forces the ground.

The Funeral of Sonny Bono
Live on CNN

It takes & turns the groove
to you, for you, for the moment is
always yours & never clear
is made to taste the powder
that sprung up deep camp dear/order
doll forever & delectable into
which
we have it now it's ours to
cherish & swell the topography
be half then beehive to
strange voices three at five
like
the carrot nose
on the snowman eat it
Bruce xxxxxxxxx
xxxxxxxxxTwo Stop
upon the rusty sled

A Town

Any mind, shaking a bucket of blue paint,
severed from itself for a split moment
by the side of the road, broken
in joy and the year getting colder.

The burnt sky and the pheasants
drag the field corn. We all dissolve,
many to applause. With the shine
of sleep: Snow melting on rocks.

The wars going on in buildings
on shady days, and someone coming over
to watch your house burn down.

The shadows eat my body.
The moon hangs a silver storm
on a starving town.

Sympathetic Magic

I turn around
and the sunset hangs out
on a fountain of air.

Moistened with the tongue of Mary,
in the sick motions of identity.

"Oh my goodness, what a sunset I am,"
the light proclaimed, splashed
like a slogan against the west.

It was Richard Crashaw's bloody tit of Christ.

The killing thing is on,
it has the electrical sound of itself being used.

War-mesh on the winterized screen,
everyone served into the electric hum.

It sends everyone to turn on
the same river, and wait beneath the tone.

It says that "enthusiasm" is the main thing,
that that's what it's all about, forever.

All is taken for a function
on the wicked horizon.

Any bird enters the glare,
and the brain of sky explodes.

My father turns gray at his computer, and says,
"Brigitte Bardot reminds me of the electric chair."

Something is trying to sing you in reverse,
and a few stars are hanging over the movie theater.

That it seemed real once,
and you could point to places on a map.

A bird goes off
in a ringing quadrant of leftover sky,
and blows the canyon out of context.

"We didn't know there was a madman in the coalition,
but you've got to have a coalition to do it."

The Pleiades.

The thunderclouds had splashed
a rorschach on the west.
Trees deleafing for the art class now.

A rendezvous with nothing,
the grass freshly cut.

Wandering into the fall-light shack,
political as a recurrent prayer.

Everyone taking antidepressants
and turning into the future.

It all gets so two-headed,
I can't help but believe I'm enjoying it.
Canyons could melt upon me.

The sun coming up to steal
upon your sidelong glance,
coming up on the survey sticks.

Don't worry.
Have a big motherf***ing drink.
It will be over soon.

Somewhere in July

1.
I was eating fried rice with "sea objects,"
and stirring in the moon, so aimlessly

I chewed upon it, and your glistening
cherry in the radiant sundial, day after day

the broken dawn is being pulled
toward Papua New Guinea, and obscures

the names we wore out from door to door,
and the winter that kept descending beyond them.

2.
That was the last belief we held
to, as you came back to bed,
and it was shining on you
like the morning sun on two mountain lakes,
the wind that was rattling the trees,
and the high wild grass that was growing
while our minds were being chewed
upon by the sweet crimson air,

after we'd come down
from the western trail,
carrying the corn syrup, the vitamin C,
and a name broken crosswise
in the burning chambers of the evening,
the familiarity that forces itself
onto our hopes for a skyline,
and gives shape to the salmon brunches,

and this being that we felt,
and how it was an increasingly

monotonous context for the pleasure
of the water rolling over our toes
in the trembling blue sundown,
though it also seemed to have formed
an interesting mask for you to wear
over your crotch, and rose, and out

of this paradigm, the knowledge
of the hangover as we felt it then
was more than simply unbecoming,
calling that sane which was really
only the same day lived over again,
and that it was only the day's makeup
which made everything seem as though it,
or we, couldn't have been real,

even if only for a moment,
and then you slept all weekend once—

Wait a minute—

There's a spider crawling on my shirt—

3.
How enchanted have you become
with your remote and serial landscape?
How is it able to say: Memory is regional.
Who was Caretaker X?
And what's become of his candy-apple ass?
Always talking about paintings and "the chills."

4.
You may hear a series of clicks
while you're being transferred
beneath the pepper tree. The grackles
at your feet on the faded blue lawn.

The air is like Demerol.
The clouds have been left upon
the gradual sky, and they've come
to break you up for a while, and rain.

5.
Here beneath these aquatic vines
hammering the drum-machine of air,
loosening the rock of the church
and the light that held it,
my body is drawn like a weed
out of the dogma of starlight.

And now that I feel as though I'm coming
to the end, everything around
me has begun, and I am someone
to the friendly dog in that window,
something that's barely brushed against
detonates all of this.

Move the beach out of memory
and leave it in a glass of wine.
Lean over the railing and learn patience.
The red-tailed hawk devouring its own
aerial circle reroutes the meaningless.
We are waiting here for the sun
to rise again, and our science-fiction
flag is raised.

Another Town, Somewhat Like the Previous One

I woke up in a used-car lot in San Marcos, Texas.
And there was a fire burning in the part of town
where you live.

In the lime clash where the clouds are grilling.
I took my prescription and that embering sky is
where you live.

Tiger swallowtail conglomerates the tangerine tree.
I grasp for my mud in the wicked trailer park
where you live.

Think of the perfect pharmacy on a deserted beach.
The black and purple sky, the moon rolling on the water,
and the seagulls sneering constantly.

Super-Abundance

Back in the station, the blank lord
of the miserable and lucky weird
is blanketed and backed

by a moon that was clipped out
of the bargain pages,
or rented by the hour,

bugged into
the anxiety that is felt
when the gift is useless in your mouth,

over by the reliable parts in the sheltered
context that the skylight sends,

the corn growing in the display cases,

an entire civilization too abused to read,
too exhausted to be wanton as the inverted trees,

to brush over paradise with gasoline and fall
into the tender radiating leaves,

the moon so full in your mouth tonight
while the family is being traded for back issues,

the makeshift music you manage to mount
one another's trophy with,

as it follows your hideous problems around,

as each decision is endlessly repeated
in you and acted out in front of the mirrors,
played over the loudspeakers,

sent to resemble the conformity of the makeshift,
metallic stars, the makeshift, metallic Jesus
rising in the field, waiting for you to be

turned over to the love of a spindly nation
with velvet trees, and it is waiting for you

to descend to its familiar face that repeats
the steps of the de-satirizing sun.

Avoiding Eye-Contact

A few trees are still being held
in the easing grip of this going-down
trembling blue spot. And there was

the criticism I received
when I crashed the car and now it echoes
toward one incomprehensibly

inconsequential star.

What She Said to Me

It was in the way we looked
at things, on occasion, and how
we hoped that what we felt
toward everything around us
would somehow not become a part
of what it was, or is. The sky
having been transfigured not only
by the infrared photography
it was subject to, in the next building
it was able to provoke resentment,
in the context of the joke-blue
it chanced to wear itself out in.

It doesn't matter.

You should never tell anyone
those things about your past.

You shouldn't have, or manufacture,
an ending that is as clear as that,
even if it were about to present itself
that way to you, in order to confuse you,
or even to forsake you, to raise
the tenements in the lackluster sun,
and to dilute any compensation you may
be able to derive from a walk in the woods.

She just took off her clothes and said,
"Without knowing what you may have done,
or even are, these trees sway
in the same tired old song about heaven."

I'll admit that I was drunk.

Maybe they do know.

Repetition with Facilitators

Not unlike the poppies in their pale
green helmets, or the sucker's lament
for the corroded green movie at happy hour,
the sun spreading a false pink devil
of teenage flesh on the lush remaindered hills,

or it is falling like a pile of cleaned bass,
one with a deranged smirk, it is calling
the moon down to languish in your mouth,
and lead you with the same loaded question:
Will anything simmer this thing on?

And penetrate the obsession as it approaches?
The trucks rolling through a wide, surly sunset
about to collide with the prayer-bells,
while you find your static corner to eat
a cucumber salad, and rehearse it to tatters?

Whether it be in the dining cars, the mimeographs,
or the mawkish arid wilderness that is nothing
but someone else's opinion you must sit through,
that it may be necessary to accept
a certain amount of patterned artificiality
framing your existence in order to burnish
the evening and better the wretched lot
of a few others, even if ever so slightly,

though about this, I'm not really sure,
but it may give you something to consider
while you're succumbing to an old issue
of the *ARP* at a café in Chiang Mai,
drinking a pineapple shake,

and wearing off on one another
after "trekking with Pong,"

as though each time the chain was yanked,
you were bound to brush up against
four or five old experiences,

the rust of which is worn into the leaves,
and into the liner-notes that open
the empty student's eye
as it is being tacked upon
the wired horizon.

A Mass-Marketing Strategy

We drove for miles through the seemingly endless
array of blue-grass mandalas, toward the fields
of what we wanted to feel and be able to call
"the second floor without longing," and the hope

that something natural might hold us there,
the hope that abandons the censors living out the film
burning inside you, with stray animals of early light
marking the far reaches of the interior,

as though that could really place you there,
systematically phone-stoned as being
radically unalone, wondering what vocal imprecisions
might serve to unzip you and take you back,

not that it can ever be the same as it once was,
but a soothing familiarity might attach itself
to certain moments, mainly at sundown,
while watering the fat leaves of the rubber plant

or wagering the guesthouses at home, in Timetable Falls,
unshuttered before the radiant stamp of eternity
and reading Rilke in the late afternoon,
with a bottle of Valium and slices of pineapple

on a lip-blue plate, it couldn't seem further away
from the necessities of life and relationships
scrawled on an emerald postcard from Wat Phrae Kew,
or a weird cat lapping yogurt from a fingerbowl,

we'll claim it's a world in which the reeds
have always swayed without the weekend winds,
ping-pong incarnates daily near the pear-shaped
swimming pool, laminating the glaze on each eyeball

as capriciously as this pre-Colombian sky
indulges the whims of each surly customer
who strolls to the cage and recites
the Eighth Elegy to the monkeys therein.

Does the Way I Sleep Make You Angry?

The river is actually glistening
and a fish pops out.
All disjointed: sky, water,
and sinking eye.

"It's called *The Auction*," she said.

That's the problem with influence,
downtown covered in parking meters.
And buckets of paint
being dumped on the new sky.

Are you watching the road?
"Do you mean this one?"

The sudden ecstasy of the people
as the sumac takes out hell in September.

What has happened to the moon?
Can anything help you to reassemble?

"I wish there was some way
to make it seem meaningful," she said.
"Instead of just making an ass
out of yourself all the time."

"Where should I park?"

Over there,
in the panic grass.

Phony Blueprints

These were what was left
of the shaggy dying trees
after winning in Las Vegas,

having walked out beyond
the sheen on its desert page

to where the popular talons
tear at the fiction
of the wet central lawn,

here beneath the gaudy overpass
at Last Canyon exit
in a fractured coral light,

the sky is canned salmon
and reindeer marrow,

open the lid or crack a bone,
and it may fill out the hours
as they fall upon you,

the water hanging
in stagnant pools near the door
with chemically-coded numbers,

this is only one idea
of your head going
over these rough red hills

and then left to spin
in a government field,

this is where we've set up
your tent and the closed-circuit TV,

and whatever is left
to formulate you further

upon the wired branches
of the faith-healer's tree.

Late Food and Early Light

1.

They were the models, the painters, and the owners,
and as dawn smashed its blazing skull on the camp,
it was certain to remake its mask of approaching light,
and work additional material into the worn minutes
being spread like a banner denouncing the rumors

of easy nonchalant days without number to follow,
and, truly enough, the persistent demands for gruesome
and ritual execution to be played out in the deep
and unaccountably plain interior had steadily increased,
and many claimed not only to welcome these developments,

but were said to have witnessed the spectacle themselves
and to have found it richly satisfying, though it should
be noted that as they were about to move their families
into the green cage, there was an unmistakable hint
of hysteria in their collective tone, issuing forth.

2.

There were hunters on stage wearing thermal underwear
in a sort of camouflage pattern, and they were pleading
with one another to behave, at least until the lights
fell, or we came to lose all sense of doubt concerning
the necessity of torn deer, the shards of Wild Turkey
bottles, or anything at all that may have been moving

through each viewer's grass mirror, but the airplane
still hasn't touched down, and it is much later for each
leaf that falls through your head, as you are flying above
the scenic carbon groves with a cool drink, and it seems
as though this sinister lobby is nothing but an experiment
in identity I've been endlessly waiting in, for you to land.

3.

What had been thinking you was nothing really but a river
rising into the dawn, as everything else had dried out
in the searing warmth of the fire that was built nearby
before you were born, as the flames leap into these steady
regulated patterns out here in the crass, hyphenated field
that the company operates as a loss-leader, like the memory

of a liquid god that leads you gently away from the notion
of finding yourself recklessly appearing on the front page,
in the incredible light that rusts the thin metal leaves
bound into the magazine, or in a picture of you standing
by the hall-tree, Mother, in the thought that your thoughts
might continue in a reversed heartbeat, all the weird movies

you came to me wearing at night, all the wildly exaggerated
scarves we like to wear out here in Tyvek Hills, the wires
that wound themselves around my small head and held out
the shot-mirror, and all the topics we had to go through
before we were finally able to get to you: that God again,
the gelatinous light again, and the sound this water makes

as it laps against a brain, and if you were to talk to this
and try to tell it something, like "It must be that the
stars in their minds have all disappeared," then it might
begin to believe in both of us, though still, the insiders
will continue to show up, intentionally, and collect large
salaries for being insufferable creeps, just as the light

begins to fall over the burnt edges of our fuzzy dreams,
which, like leaves, hang briefly in the mouth of the autumn
wind, and the others are incapable of listening to anything
anyone else ever says, though they are only people talking
about the people they had listened to on talk-shows, and you
know that it shouldn't really bother you, so why let it?

Coming To in South Korea

Even as though it was really only
happening in the song on the radio,
on this bus that is careening
through the black and blue landscape,
through the floating eye of the rainwater,
and through each formal occasion
in which the paper dolls are silently
hung from the flying trees
and asked a series of questions
about the burnt images that we spend
each day forcing one another to recall,
to spread ourselves out before
the church like two wobbling sunsets,
as though it was about to begin
again and let me understand,
if it was to turn into you, saying,
"Fun isn't what it used to be,"
in that it can no longer make anything
seem truly uncertain, as the designer
hillside slurs under the weight
of systematic relief: I've just decided
to give everyone some Xanax for Christmas,
the burning leaves, the cardboard sunbathers,
the previous woods you had worn out
on the tip of your loose tongue
were turning back upon you, as if to say,
"The air has that hammered-on feel,"
and it's like staying awake throughout
your entire shift and staring absently
at the camellias, and to come apart
for the delight of any unsettling moment,
though just as suddenly your spirit falls
into the predictable order of the interaction
as another diabolic rose blooms in the iron
lung of the conversation you have to keep,

as it lets each ruined tongue burn slowly
while a gray face in the wild remains,
with an old fork, and each sound that tried
to shed its skin, as though it could
conceal and then recreate the world
that it claimed to be touching,
between each burning doll.

At the Tianjin Grand Hotel

It was so very event-like,
even if it was only a few plants
in bloom along the path,

it splayed me like the memory
of you standing next to a U-Haul
out on the frozen lawn,

as though saying it
could make it happen,

and not only once
but in numerous strange outfits,

in which case tomorrow
may be Friday, with a sail raised
into the center
of its corrupt angelic heart,

it's beautiful all the same
though isn't it?

It's not life, really, but it is
thinking its way toward it,

like a metal price-tag
staggering in the wind.

Drink this soft glass of milk
as though you were about to
throw out everything you'd think
you might ever need.

And, sure enough,
here you are,
with your knees bent,
looking into the lost face of it.

Still

If we go on like this forever,
and to the hills,
which are a whale-skin blue
in the antisocial hours,

mist on the ridge like a glass headache,
and the robbers an hour beyond
the random liquor store have each ordered
the Biggie Fries and the Biggie Coke,

then it will only be the sky lit at night
that beats your head against a wall
of belief, and it is only life that evaporates
into work that is useless though the sponsors

sing it affectionately, then you will
go into the predictability and won't think
to panic, and when you wake up,
only half of the room will be startling.

The Full Night Still in the Street Water

A storm came down, it is only dripping now,
it caught steel cords in the lumberyard
near the window, it ricocheted a charge

through the television and set the body
nerve on bone; I went to wander on corners
supercilious, to feel age on my tongue

like blue particles making concision
of apposition, something burning from a cut
in a stone wall meant expansion

of capital, what was once
surrender; i.e., gets off the horse and lies
down in the autumn dust

of maple trees, crunching the red
massacre of leaves, this was
a memory of going down, looking out the door.